A Locket of

of

Forever Love

DEDICATION

To every chosen child—
your journey is a celebration of love's
power to create family.
Here's to
belonging, love, and the families we make.

Emily (or Em as she was often called) lived a happy life with her Mom, her Dad, and her younger brother, Jake. With her curly brown hair and twinkling brown eyes, Emily was a silly, playful, happy girl. The family often went on picnics, played board games, and even had weekly ice cream.

Jake, Emily's little brother was a cutie with his short, blonde hair, big blue eyes and chubby cheeks, was the center of the family.

Emily loved him and loved being a big sister.

Daddy gave Emily a small, golden-wrapped box. Emily carefully unwrapped it to find a beautiful locket that had "Forever Love" etched into it.

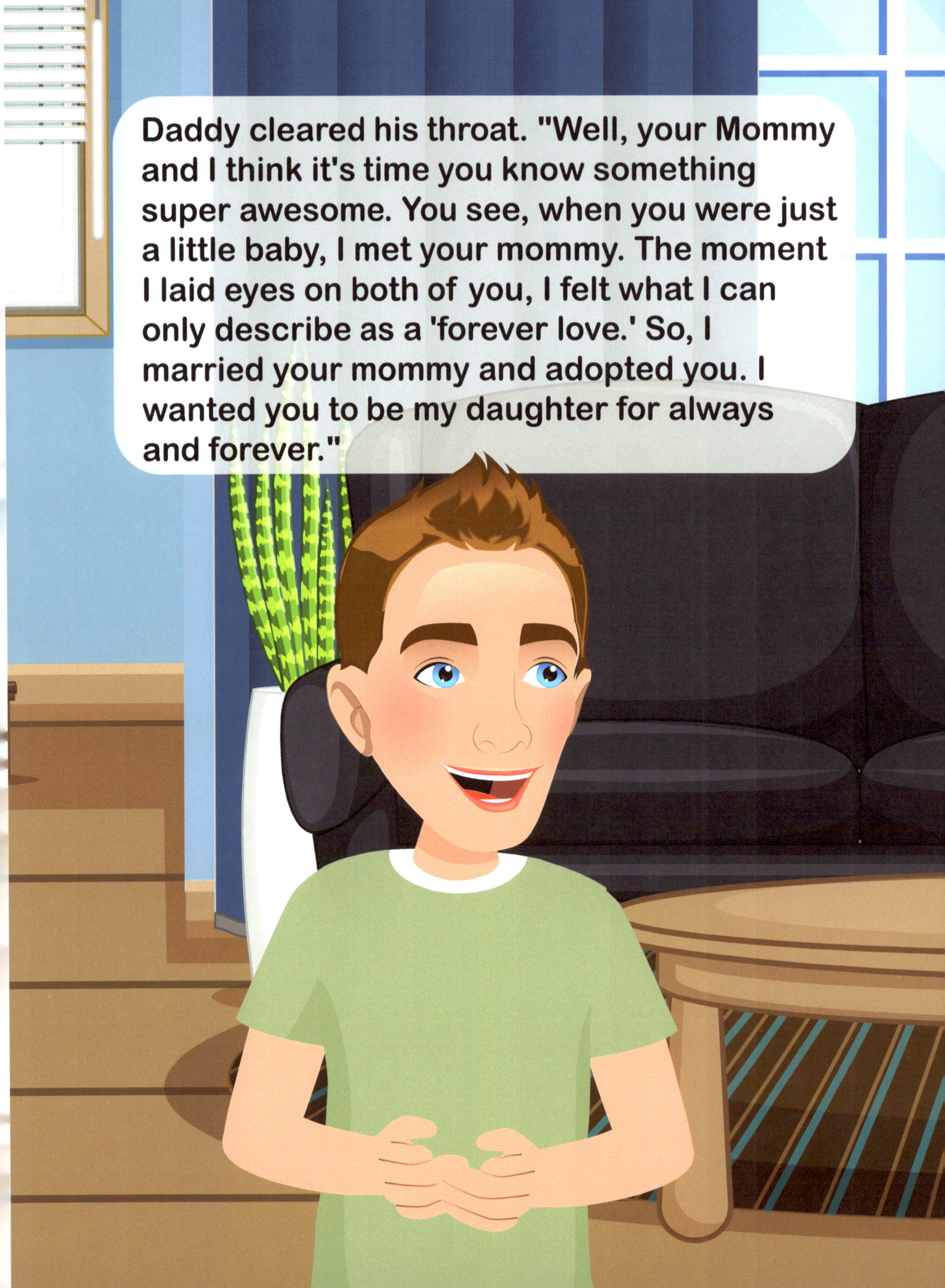

Emily looked confused. "Adopted? But you're my daddy. Why would you have to adopt me?" Daddy tilted his head a bit, smiling, "Being a Daddy isn't about being there from the very start, It's about choosing to love and care for you every single day. I got to choose to be your Daddy. And it's the best choice I ever made."

"What about Jake? Did you adopt him too?", she asked

"But Jake is your 'real' son, right? Do you love him more?" Emily looked up, her eyes starting to fill with tears.

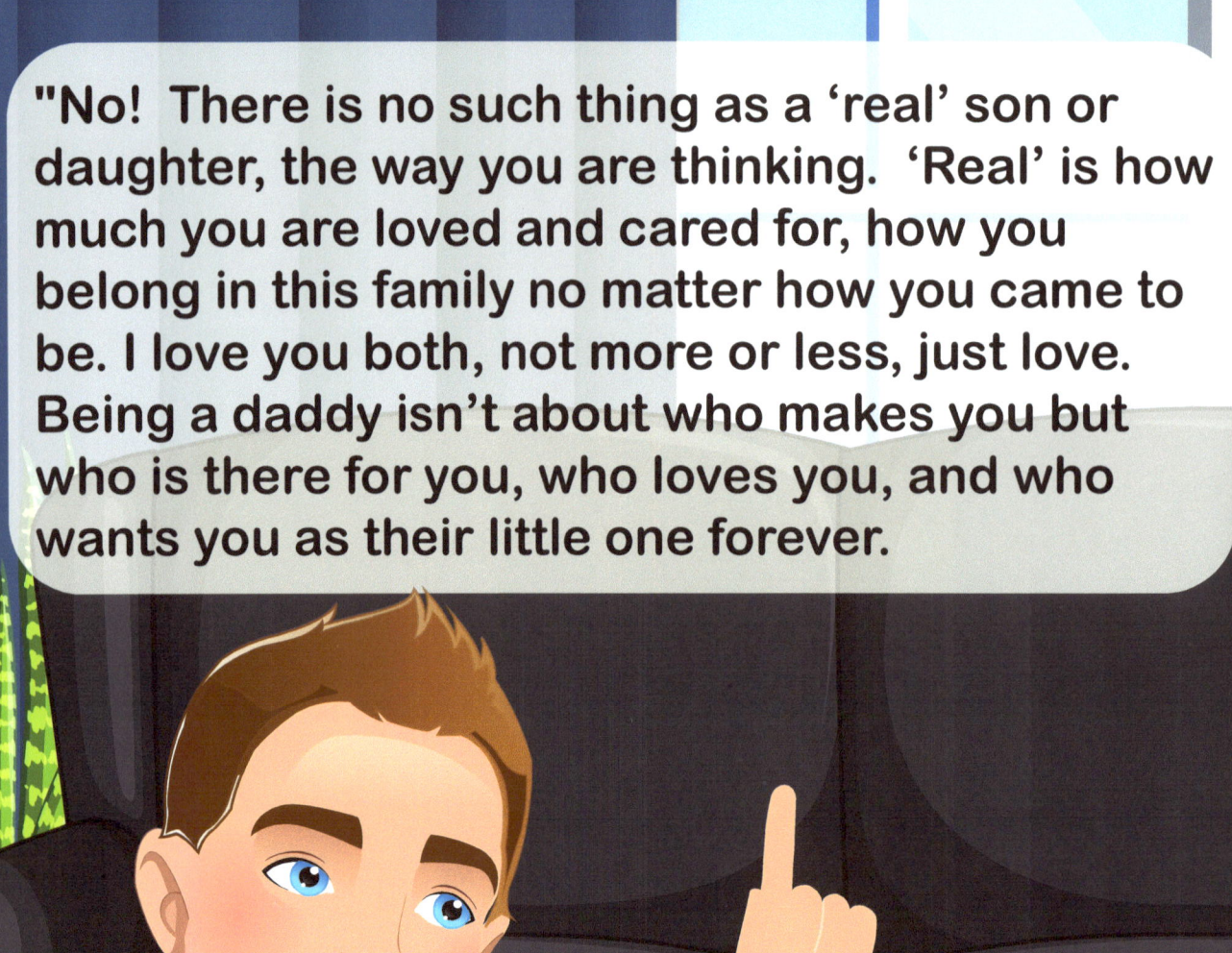

"No! There is no such thing as a 'real' son or daughter, the way you are thinking. 'Real' is how much you are loved and cared for, how you belong in this family no matter how you came to be. I love you both, not more or less, just love. Being a daddy isn't about who makes you but who is there for you, who loves you, and who wants you as their little one forever.

"Of course I will! We are a family and we are going to be here for each other always. Families are more than blood or how you came to be; they are about loving each other completely and unconditionally." Daddy said, pulling her into a big hug that surrounded her with his loving arms.

Back home, Emily squeezed her locket that hung around her neck. She then hugged Daddy tightly and said, "I love you, Daddy. I'm happy you chose me."

"And I will always choose you, Emily. We have a forever love, and that will never change," Daddy hugged her back tight and they both knew they are family and their love would last forever.